Paul Durcan was born in D ...., iviayo
parents, and studied archaeology and medieval history at
University College Cork. His first book, *Endsville* (with Brian
Lynch), appeared in 1967, and has been followed by 14 others,
including *Teresa's Bar* (1976), *Sam's Cross* (1978), *Jesus, Break
His Fall* (1980), *Jumping the Train Tracks with Angela* (1983), *The
Berlin Wall Café* (Poetry Book Society Choice, 1985), *Going
Home to Russia* (1987), *Daddy, Daddy* (1990), *Crazy about
Women* (1991) and *A Snail in My Prime: New and Selected Poems*
(1993). In 1974 he won the Patrick Kavanagh Award and in
1978 and 1980 received Creative Writing Bursaries from the
Arts Council/An Chomhairle Ealaíon, Ireland. Apart from
Britain and Ireland, he has also read in the former Yugoslavia,
the former Soviet Union, the USA (where in 1985 he was res-
ident poet at The Frost Place, New Hampshire), Canada
(including the 1995 Vancouver International Writers Festival),
Holland (at the Rotterdam International Poetry Festival),
France, Italy, Luxembourg, Belgium, New Zealand (Writers'
and Readers' Week), Israel and, in 1995, Germany and Brazil.
In October 1989 he received the Irish American Cultural
Institute Poetry Award and in 1990 won the Whitbread Poetry
Award with *Daddy, Daddy*. In the same year he was Writer in
Residence at Trinity College Dublin. His most recent book is
*Give Me Your Hand* (1994), a sequence of poems inspired by
paintings in London's National Gallery. He was jointly
awarded the Heinemann Bequest, 1995, by the Royal Society
for Literature. He is a member of Aosdána and lives in Dublin.

*Paul Durcan*

# O WESTPORT
# IN THE LIGHT
# OF ASIA MINOR

THE HARVILL PRESS
LONDON

*O Westport in the Light of Asia Minor* first published 1975
by Anna Livia Books, Dublin
*Endsville* first published 1967 by New Writers Press, Dublin

This revised edition of *O Westport in the Light of Asia Minor*
incorporating poems from *Endsville*
first published 1995 by
The Harvill Press
84 Thornhill Road
London N1 1RD

A CIP catalogue record for this title is available from
the British Library

ISBN 1 86046 087 9

ACKNOWLEDGEMENTS
Acknowledgements are gratefully made to the editors of *Adam International Review*;
*Aquarius* (London); *Arena*; Hayden Murphy's *Broadsheet*; *The Bunbrosna Stream*; *Choice*;
*The Copper Journal*; *The Dublin Magazine*; *General Vallancey's Bridge*; *Goldsmith Poetry
Calendar*; *Hibernia*; *The Holy Door*; *Icarus* (TCD); *The Lace Curtain*; *New Irish Writing* (The
Irish Press); *Nine Queen Bees* (Honolulu); *The Pleiades Will Burst into Tears*; *The Pleiades
Will Weep over Douglas Hyde*; *Poetry Ireland Pyramid* (Massachusetts); *Quarryman* (UCC); *St
Stephens* (UCD); *Structure; Threshold*; *Two Rivers*; and *The Wearing of the Black* (Belfast).

Typeset in Monophoto Bembo by
Servis Filmsetting Ltd, Manchester

Printed and bound in Great Britain by
Butler & Tanner, Frome, Somerset

TO NESSA O'NEILL

What has passed, has gone;
What is past, will come.

MARTIN HEIDEGGER


from which ever child-crib within whatever enclosure
demarked by a dynast or staked by consent
wherever in which of the wide world-ridings
              you must not call her but by that name
which accords to the morphology of that place.

DAVID JONES

# AUTHOR'S NOTE

When *O Westport in the Light of Asia Minor* was published in 1975 it incorporated one poem from *Endsville* (1967) – "Animus Anima Amen". I am glad to be able to restore this poem to the work from *Endsville* which I wish to retain as well as to re-publish the poems in *O Westport in the Light of Asia Minor* in their proper sequence. *Endsville* was a joint publication with Brian Lynch and its epigraph was from Hart Crane's *Voyages:* "And could they hear me, I would tell them".

# CONTENTS

*from* ENDSVILLE

I

# Nessa

I met her on the First of August
In the Shangri-La Hotel,
She took me by the index finger
And dropped me in her well.
And that was a whirlpool, that was a whirlpool,
And I very nearly drowned.

Take off your pants, she said to me,
And I very nearly didn't;
Would you care to swim, she said to me,
And I hopped into the Irish Sea.
And that was a whirlpool, that was a whirlpool,
And I very nearly drowned.

On the way back I fell in the field
And she fell down beside me,
I'd have lain in the long grass with her all my life
With Nessa:
She was a whirlpool, she was a whirlpool,
And I very nearly drowned.

O Nessa my dear, Nessa my dear,
Will you stay with me on the rocks?
Will you come for me into the Irish Sea
And for me let your red hair down?
And then we will ride into Dublin City
In a taxi-cab wrapped up in dust.
Oh you are a whirlpool, you are a whirlpool,
And I am very nearly drowned.

# Gate 8

*for Nessa*

Lean your behind on the departure gate
For to clown out of the wound of separation
With Ali smile and Ali shuffle:
Such was the advice and such was how
We kept each other from feeling low.

What do you make of the Bunny Beds I mean
The Bunny Clubs? Tails
I love you, heads I don't. The dead
Are pure was what my father said
The night he swapped his wife for lead.

I am afraid to ask if they are the shoes
Bought you by your mother yesterday.
FLIGHT 118 TO LONDON: BOARDING NOW.
Come to London: I will, I will.
And the poet's stone fell up the hill.

Is there no end to corridors?
Thank God you did not turn to wave.
They would not allow me on the roof
So right then I took a return coach
Into the darkening city.

Rain and the streets emptied
Of people and you.
What am I to think?
Of the man inside the TV man
Propped on the seat behind

Tell-telling the outside man
To produce *The Playboy of the Western World*
On an ice rink with an all-negro cast?
Yes and of no and the sky
That holds you now. I doubt

If you love me and . . . you know
My footwork's not good and my eyes cut bad.

# On a BEA Trident Jet

The shadows of the Pyrenees on the clouds,
Husbands awake about sleeping wives,
These are the regions beyond calculation,
Your wife is sleeping because she is your wife.

A marriage is a March overture to superstition
And then when you lose it – your life –
And pieces of it are washed up on some foreign shore
People will know it was yours.

# Lines Written Three Miles from Watershed Island

Sand martins helicoptering into the upper air
Are like the Nerves of Lovers
Hovering over them as Advertisements of Awkwardness;
O writer, do not turn them into god and goddess;
Humanity is bottomless if the truth be loved.

She is unity of being –
The fire in her his new hands now may kindle
And she builds her limbs around him, making a sea-grove
Inside of which he kneels a grown boy out-grown by a
    mountain tree
And upon her roots he pours all the water.

The tree sinks down into the climbing earth;
Now he may lay his head upon the roots he died for.
She moves her branches, secreting shadows that in long lengths
    fall through his head;
Her face is her soul –
Inside the outside like a tree.

Sand martins drop down through the lower air
As over sand hills through dusk under starlight
A young pair tramp homeward to parent and child.

# In the Springtime of Her Life My Love Cut off Her Hair

She rat-tat-tatted on the glass-paned door of our flat-roofed
    suburban home
And I unlatched it with much faith as ever and before;
But when I saw what she had done I knew pain to the myelitic
    bone
And saw that all I had written and worked for was no more.
For what Keats said of his long poem was true of my love's
Auburn hair – smoke in autumn but redder
Than down-goings of carrot suns on summer's eves –
"A place to wander in" in figures-of-eight along somnambulent
    rivers.
From that day on – in April cruel as ever –
A figure-of-eight was severed and I am sleepless
In a Chinese prison of all-human loneliness
In which I cannot sleep but think, think of her
As she was and – cut off from the Tree of Life – ignobly pine.
I loved her for her auburn hair and not herself alone.

# The Daughters Singing to Their Father

Now he will grope back into the abode and crouch down;
Another dry holocaust in the suburban complex over;
Over another stagger home along the semi-detached gauntlet;
Another day done. It has never not been,
Not even on worse days when only grave-dark was craved for.
He will crouch down and whether the night
Be starry or not
He will behold no stillness take shape upon his knees;
Nor rainbow book nor snow-white cat;
Nor will that woman of women, fire of fires – the one of the
    old smile
Breaking out in sheet gold in her cave-red hair –
Hover near, nor turn the page over
For her votary in the broken chair.
No matter what bedlam or vacuum the night may rear
He will hear only his daughters singing to him
From behind the arabic numerals of the clock:
"There is no going back, boy, there is no going back."
Long will he gaze into the clock, and to that last spouse
Under the skyline – for his daughters give thanks.

# Hymn to Nessa

*Climbing back over to zero*
*I nearly fell over the sea;*
*Climbing back over to zero*
*The sea fell over me.*

Behind me on the sea shore Nessa lay;
She is the red sun at nightfall.
Behind me on the sea shore Nessa lay;
Watching me walk out to sea.

I looked back and saw her wave towards me;
She burned through her eyes.
I looked back and saw her wave towards me;
Her face burning in coals.

Behind her a cliff stood with grass on it;
She lay at the base of the cliff.
Behind her a cliff stood with grass on it;
She waved from the base of the cliff.

She waved and she waved and she waved;
She lay down and shuttered her eyes.
She waved and she waved and she waved;
Shuttering her eyes in the sun.

When I looked back again she was not gone;
She was sleeping under the sun.
When I looked back again she was not gone;
She was sleeping under the sun.

II

# O Westport in the Light of Asia Minor

## I

Feet crossed, arms behind his head,
God lay below the skyline hidden from sight;
And Gauloise smoke trailed up the sky.

British frocks and dresses lay draped on the rocks,
Grey flashing windows of a nineteenth-century boutique,
While on the sands the girls lay lazily on their sides
All moon in the daylight
Musing "What is he like?" but at the back of their minds
The heart raged on:
Flame seamed with all the scorn of a soldier
Saying "After the battle".

## II

But often the Reek would stand with a cloud round its head;
Behind the sky stood God with a cleaver raised;
Yet when cocky men peered round the curtain of sky
There was no god and the mists came,
Lay down on the west coast,
Fur off the back of a graveyard,
As if an ape had got the tedium of a thousand years between his
    maulers
And shoved it across the world onto our land:
The mists put the fear of our mother into us:
I am what I am for fear of hiding in the action
And yet –

If this world is not simply atmosphere pierced through and
    through
With the good doubt,

Then here it was Red Riding Hood who was laid up in bed;
It was Red-Eared Black Tongue who crouched at the bedside;
And she did the child no harm but good.

But there were some who had guts, took action and stayed;
And standing on the mountains of their dread saw
The islands come up through the mists –
Seductive garments that a man might dream of –
And with the islands finally the sun;
Black at the edges, pure red at the centre.

They came at a run down the mountain
Landing with such falls that even the few small hard gold pieces
    in their pockets
Smashed into pieces so infinitesimal that not even a Shylock ever
    would find them;
They came starting out of their breeches out onto the stony
    shore,
The sea was a great unnamed flower whose leaves they stood
    under
And danced to ring upon ring;
Thin prickly bearded men casting ridiculousness to the
    multitude,
Casting in great armfuls made bountiful by the slow and graceful
    whirling of their arms,
And they sang: "As if a rock were naked."

# Turlough

*for William and Ann*

Wake up once more in Turlough, trawl the sun
For the red at twilight and her coal black veil;
Glimpse through these broad green leaves that trail
Down your eyes a sole-yellow kingdom.
This daybreak is a round tower
In whose eyes crouch fliers of the six-foot deep.
Let the winds pour
Until our very sides themselves do weep
And our punched heads flower out of laughter.
It is for her passing that we woo her.
And when in the afternoon, late and gone, all the windows
Of the townland are laid out in rows
The river leaps to pronounce its blessing
And the young men change with the girls and the tower comes
    down.

# Letter to Sailorson

And now that we are outside Creation
We are inmates of Invention:
I must not, on a stroll through the park,
On a day off from school,
Say the object I saw gleaming like a feeling
Was my soul.
It was, I would be more favoured to report,
A flying saucer or, more favoured still,
An unstable horse ghosted by my mother.
Ask women who God is, they say:
"A spook in specs with a napkin on his nut."

My birthday, says the earth, is the last day in June,
The crossroads at evening where you went to
When, like heaven, you were seven skies high;
So high – I could see in the window
And the harmonicas igniting
The china canes we caught beneath the moon –
The smooth, the cold, the slender, bamboos of the daylight
    moon.

London here is a chapped hen broody on a pill;
But Mayo June is where I am, this afternoon in April.
In where are you?
A scarf, a great coat, and a dancing shoe.
Salut.

# Aughawall Graveyard

Lonely lonely lonely lonely:
The story with a middle only.

# Crazy Cradle Bay

The son of Eoin is a fisherman
Who sleeps while his mates fish.
He's the man who delivers the final blows
When the nets are emptied on the pier at dawn.
His father, the shopkeeper, charges sixpence
For a fivepenny ice cream.
His wife is as clean as she's lean
And his mother remembers you in her dreams.
But if you down twelve pints in Rafters Rest
You too might see the ghosts
Of the sons of the son of Eoin
Walking the waters of Crazy Cradle Bay.

# Rough Love in Jericho

"Christ, it is lonely in this house."
He looked over at the clock
But could not recall if he had set it fast or slow.
"At any rate –
Somewhere in the middle of a Sunday afternoon."
He looked out the window at the rain
And the whins on fire.
Mayo – yellow even on a black day.
"I enjoyed the few pints
In spite even of that lie I told
About having cheese back in the house."

The stream at the back of the field began to rise
Making a bright dark cave he crouched in
And he saw a woman whose name he did not know
But that she was a mother gleamed from her
And, moreover, there was an infant on her knee.
How could she have known that twenty years would find
That so tiny inside-out born-of-famine body
Desperate on London streets –
That picking at random a first passer-by
He would unclench his jacket to expose a hatchet
And seethe: Two quid or I'll split your head open.
How could she have known? And yet her face was pock marked
With tears.

He awoke and laid his hand on his heart
Just as he'd done when he'd been gone for
By the boy with the hatchet
Under the bridge at Ladbroke Grove Station.
"And now my wife and children are in Dublin
I'm forbidden by law to ever see them again.

The Judge said – They must be spared this man's irrational fear.
O Black Day and Fire outside my window
I will go out tonight and the first mansion in the town of
    Westport that I come to
I will tear it down brick by brick until they take me away saying:
    Tell that to the Taoiseach.
So help me Anthony. And then maybe I'll help you with stories
    of Rough Love in Jericho."

# Ballina, Co Mayo

*for Sailorson*

It is the last town before the river meets the sea.

At evening in summertime young men and old men
Stand on the bridge watching the waters flow under them,
    under the arches;
They lean their elbows on the wall with their hands cupped, as
    though in prayer;
But though they may in themselves be kneeling
They are standing squarely on the callous pavement.
The air is full of reasonableness –
If their own faces float past them they are not bothered,
They do not dwell or harp on it;
And if at their life's end they whisper for a priest
It may be because of what they can hear among all these waters'
    silences and sounds
Such as the matchstick that being borne along helplessly upon
    the waters
Is seeming to say: *Let this chalice pass from me* . . .
Or, it should be reported, making the sound that those words
    make
And, how can we not say, with meaning too:

Poor Splinter trapped in the emotion –

III

# Outside the Church of the Descent of the Holy Ghost

Hosanna to the young woman in the long black rain coat
Ascending the church steps on an afternoon in winter!
I did not doubt the deliberation with which she weaved
A sensual path into the black shadows of the porch
And yet how frail a creature
That now was minutely flying headlong into the Wall of God.

But I had but two eyes on her, for behind me
Between the sunlight and the snow
Came a small family out for their Sunday walk;
A family just like any other family
Except for the Alsatian dog prancing beside them:
Geoffrey, I heard them call, Geoffrey, Geoffrey.

Now safe from that small family for a time at least
I think of you – young woman on the church steps –
Of how families are made – or not made –
Of how I am my daughters' father and I pray
May they not inherit the world of the family
And the murderous animal of possession.
Dear nameless woman, suntrap, scarp of snow,
If you should see the hawthorn blossom on a day in winter
Relish the actuality, do not flinch from pain.

# Poem for My Father

He could feel, as he lay half-awake on his mat,
Not knowing if it were night or day,
The same black space behind the ears,
*My nightmare is my family*, and these hands of mine
Would wrench off my shoulders if they could,
But I am as the waters of my fate,
My father plunging through them to become me.

Outside, a commuter, refugee, goes leaping along the street
As by his fingertips he clings
To the broken glass of a late winter twilight sky.
Marked man, face up against the sky,
Riddled with aspirations.

II

I saw through my fingers a man in the sky
Moving out the bay:

Reality's Jack swaying out to sea.

What need to look back
Into the night at the root of it?
Who grips the twine to a poor man's kite
Grips me.

# Tibidabo

At the carnival on the hill I stand at a balcony gazing down
On the papas of Barcelona putting their kids through the Maze;
And I listen to the howl until I know not where I am
And, for fear of falling out of my terror, grip tight the rails.

Survival and I retreat back into the cave in the skull of the hill
Crazed with the slot-machine puppet shows, clashing;
And even though the instruction says FOR CHILDREN ONLY
I put the peseta into the machine called El Inferno:

And the darkness became a light on the darkness
On whose gilded waters flanked by palace walls
Proceeded brother and sister treading the family circle from
    eternity.
In a minute it is all over and I put in the second peseta.

# I Saw the Father in the Daughter's Eyes

*for Martin Green*

I saw the father in the daughter's eyes
And his father's face in his and
I saw the world begin to spin and spin
And when she said: "I may as well go home"
I said: "You may as well go home."

But then when she had gone
The machinery crashed to a halt
And I was dazed and the table ached
And I was in a cafeteria
Where all the creatures at the formica tables ached:

Ached until it appeared we were being all split up
And up the aisle in a whisper chanting
Came a black man, the nonchalance of whose swerve
Upset me – to the roots of the groin –
And he was saying: "I am my memory, I am my memory."

# Prothalamium

*for John O'Neill and Ann Hughes, 2 September 1971*

*. . . to be spoken at the moment of your marriage*
*by a man on the road near to Blessington*

"staying is nowhere"
RAINER MARIA RILKE

Whenever I have felt close to reality
I have felt faint beyond all self-pity.

Is not "staying" where the Liffey leapt through a gap
To be pinned thereby to a Heavenly Map?

Where now the white flame leaps between you both
To join your eyes upon its rocky path?

# Words for a Marriage

*to Mark Wickham and Mary Murphy, 15 August 1974*

In the days of your courtship you doubted
That a swan could nest in a place with no shelter,
On a bar of sand near a grotesque oil tanker,
And survive, and as the weeks unravelled
You kept returning to the island to make doubly certain
Until came a day she was gone –
Only naturally shattered egg shells remaining.
Now in the days of your marriage friends celebrating
Wonder how two people unusually fearless and gentle
Can marry like this, and survive, and the cliffhanging case
For your friends is that they know you will;
Dream like a mantilla drawn back from the face
Of reality, cygnets ferried safely on her back
In flight through even ill-winds, white through black.

# Wife Beats Husband at Sligo Festival

"The festival had him killed, all festivals
Have him killed
Or else Your Lordship, he says,
Must consider him an accident merely
As indeed a French philosopher is said to have taught
His own child as a prayer: *I am an accident merely* etc. etc.
He says that he believes in festivals
And that he understood what kind of pole it was that all the
    people including his own wife
Were dancing around, hopping and stopping.
The pole, he says, was a corner
Into which he had escaped from his dreams,
A corner of the square,
And that he understood also that a maypole in the end must
    fall."
Haste to the Wedding.

# Plato Lucy's Furniture Arcade

Proud of her sleeping husband, she lies awake
Inhaling the nicotine of his manure-brown hands,
Stench of hair oil and pints-of-porter tang;
She smiles at a hundred memories of his bandy legs
In snow-white briefs or outsize morning suit,
His squinting eyes on sunny day at seaside,
His freshly furrowed brow on wedding day;
And she hears from the farthest strand of all the world
His deep sea voice break softly on the shore.

And as she lies there beside her sleeping lord
Likewise lie his schemes inside his head
To stock with music his furniture arcade,
And divans-for-two and cut-price double-beds;
She's Plato's wife at Plato's great parade.

# General Vallancey's Waltz

*for A.K.*

I'm a Westmeath solicitor long lost in Peking, long, lost, and
    forgotten,
And I used to sit up in my hall late into the night listening for
    *you*;
But it was not enough, it was not enough,
So I sailed up the Liffey from China,
Back to the wall, back to the wall,
To Liberty Hall.

I got married in due course, to a good Peking lass, of good
    Communist stock,
But she turned turkey on me, said she needed more money,
That there was not enough, that there was not enough,
So I sailed up the Liffey from China,
Back to the wall, back to the wall,
To Liberty Hall.

Oh forgive me my shout if I fall through your easy chair,
    through the back of your easy chair,
My knees are the crux of the world's local problem, no knees –
    no heaven;
Oh but there *is* all in all, there *is* all in all,
So I sailed up the Liffey from China,
Back to the wall, back to the wall,
To Liberty Hall.

# Brighton Beach

Have you ever watched the sea go out at Brighton
And known that you were not going with it too;
And the grey horizon putting up the shutters
And wished you were behind them long ago?

For it is blue by night in Normandy
And Normans are by morning fairer still
And stick, as they walk out the day at noon,
Red feathers in the yellow fields of time.

Have you ever watched your bare-armed grey-haired mother
And she is in the garden hanging out
Your shirt, and your father's on the clothesline?
From Brighton that is the horizon that I see.

And on the shore deserted as that room
That every child has to make her own
I stand behind the windows of my eyes
As the sea is blown away by the winding gulls.

# On a June Afternoon in Saint Stephen's Green

With Macdara I found myself walking
Behind a young woman in her light summer wear.
If we were walking, she was riding
The clear waters of her cotton dress
And I thought: had I the choice I had been a woman –
Instead I am strung up on a cloud called mind.
Even were I to walk naked my body were a cumbersome coat.
O fortunate soul, walking on her hips through the Green.

# Serena

Nineteen forty-eight in the country,
A modest castle by the sea or some
Such cottage of height or depth
That would not trap but draw
The sunlight through the cotton veils.
The windows would be doors
And the bell would echo-echo,
Room to room, down the passage way.
Where? In Westport, I would say,
Or Greece, or Israel-in-the-fields.

But, if I may sadly say so
(I know you know the facts of death),
This is no place and the time
Is as always and more so than myself
Outrageously, simply, wrong,
Dear fleeting friend, go wear
A Neapolitan cocktail gown
At my Father's breakfast.
He's getting married in the morning, in Cana town.

# La Terre des Hommes

Fancy meeting *you* out here in the desert:
Hallo Clockface.

# Please Stay in the Family, Clovis

Please stay in the family Clovis:
The tawny curtains in the front parlour –
Though we do not use that room –
Would somehow not look quite the same
Without you – when you get married
We could put the presents in the front parlour –
Blankets pillowcases teaspoons carvers –
All in a row on the sideboard:
No better or more thoughtful present
Than a quality set of carvers, Clovis:
Why – you and Olive and (D.V.) your children
Could live here with us:
All it would mean would be a bit more cleaning
And do not snap back that I am only just dreaming:
I'm talking about reality Clovis:
And we still would not have to use the front parlour:
Love Mother.

# Palmerston Park

High summer afternoon in the drawing room,
Aunt Laura and I at the bay window,
And in the garden waltzing with the flowers
In a Symphony of Ennui – Uncle Charles.
This way and that, rich man, rich flowers,
And he would not come in
Because of one who lived there.

There was a silence when she said:
"What the Dickens is he doing out there?"
I rubbed my chin until she spoke again:
"And do you know – he once wrote a poem."

# Black Sister

Black sister with an afro halo round your head
And a handbag by your side and a string of beads,
Watching for news from a newsreel in the dark
Of the television lounge of a country hotel,
You are lean, tall and fruitful as a young beech
And seductive as the tree of knowledge
But – forgive me, this *is* the millenium to enquire –
Is that not you yourself stepping across the screen
Out of missionary fields into a country courthouse
Machine gun firing from your thigh, and freedom
On your dying lips?
*But you are whispering to me tonight:*
*O Acton, let us be ambiguous tonight.*

Instead you are cooped up in Ireland in a small hotel
Waiting for your boy whose magic daddy
Though no niggard to mission fields at Sunday Mass
Is not standing for his son to hitch up with a black bitch
Even if she's a Catholic virgin.
She's black and therefore a whore.
And electric mammy, than whom there is no more fiercesome
Drum-beater for black babies,
Collapsed when she glimpsed the sun dancing halo round your
    head.
But you're a patient girl –
While over dark deep well waters lit up by huge arc lights
*You are whispering to me tonight:*
*O Acton, let us be ambiguous tonight.*

# Horses and Tombstones

Because I loved my sister and had never thought not to
No more than I had thought to kill my father or fight my
    brother,
Deep late in the night when all were dead in bed,
I told her that although I too was made of stone
I would not cohere into even so much as a spall or a flake
Were it not for the hill streams that over me have coursed
And how, just as in winter I have dreamed of a summer's evening
    kiss,
So, once, a summer's evening in summer dreamed me with wet
    kisses
And long black arms that would wind round the orb if they
    were let.

I sang her even a few bars of my Stone's Song to the Stream
"Oh meet me in the dream" – but she would have none of it.
O my young sister of the revolution,
My young doctor with a hairband,
You only grew a beard and muttered,
Chin in hand,
"Horses and tombstones, tombstones and horses."

In the cold January dawn I climbed over felled elms
But went walking on in terror only of my sister:
I found succour in the uprooted earth
And shelter in the roofless sky.

# Phoenix Park Vespers

A man hiking the roads or tramping the streets
Has elegies for hills and epitaphs for houses
But his wife, while she has thought only for the ultimate
    destination
And is much more strict about weekly attendance at church,
Has much less belief in an afterlife or in heaven –
Thus under the conifers of the Phoenix Park,
Under the exceedingly lonely conifers of the Phoenix Park,
Under their blunt cones and amidst their piercing needles,
I squatted down and wept;
I who have but rarely shed a tear in sorrow.

The hurriedly-emptying October evening skies neither affirmed
    nor denied
A metaphysics of sex
But reflected themselves merely in the fields below
As flocks of kindred groups, courting couples, and footballers,
Old men, and babes, and loving friends,
And youths and maidens gay,
Scattered for homes.

The floor where I crouched was lit up by litters
Of the terracotta cones
And in the darkness at the heart of the wood
Kids played at giants and gnomes.
A woman (of whom I was so fond I actually told her so),
Not as a query but as a rebuke
Said to me: "What are you thinking?"
And I knew that whatever I said she would add
Half-coyly, mockingly, coaxingly:
"O my dear little *buachaillín*, but it is all one;
Enough of Baudelaire, there *is* no connection."

I think now of her face as of a clock
With the long hand passing over her eyes
But passing over backwards as well as forwards,
To and fro – like a speedometer needle.
And this long hand, where once was her hound-like nose,
At once tells the time and points a warning finger;
Warning me to bear in mind that while the cradle is but a grave
The grave is not a cradle but is for ever.
And while her iron voice clanks tonelessly away
Her face grows blacker under her heaped-over hair;
And I see that all church architecture is but coiffure
And all mystical entrances are through women's faces.
She opens her mouth and I step out onto her ice-pink tongue
To be swallowed up for ever in the womb of time.

IV

# 30 November 1967

*to Katherine*

I awoke with a pain in my head
And my mother standing at the end of the bed;
"There's bad news in the paper," she said,
"Patrick Kavanagh is dead."

After a week which was not real
At last I settled down to a natural meal;
I was sitting over a pint and a beef sandwich
In Mooney's across the street from the Rotunda.

By accident I happened to tune in
To the conversation at the table from me;
I heard an old Northsider tell to his missus
"He was pure straight, God rest him, not like us."

# They Say the Butterfly Is
# the Hardest Stroke

*to Richard Riordan*

From coves below the cliffs of the years
I have dipped into *Ulysses*,
*A Vagrant, Tarry Flynn* –
But for no more than ten minutes or a page;
For no more than to keep in touch
With minds kindred in their romance with silence.
I have not "met" God, I have not "read"
David Gascoyne, James Joyce, or Patrick Kavanagh:
I believe in them.
Of the song of him with the world in his care
I am content to know the air.

# The Nun's Bath

I drink to the middle of it all.
Between the sandhills,
The sandhills between the hayfields and the sea,
There stood a tub and in it
A buxom nun who scrubbed herself as if
The early morning air was itself the water –
A water dance that was being wound
Round her by a yellow duck.

Now here in this gruesome London pub
I make myself the middle of it all.
I know that when I stand to get my beer
Another nomad may well steal my stool;
And let the barmaid be mournful if she will.
My job is to be present which I am.
There is the day ahead with more or less agony
Than to suffer all day in the Convent of Mercy.

# Le Bal

And around John Keats and around
Life the Ballerina spun
And faster
Until she was no more than her spinning:
A delirious circumference, a freezing absence,
Inside of which – not even *he* could breathe.

# The Man Outside the *Metropole*

*for Brian Rooney*

Outside the *Metropole*
I stood like Wallace Stevens
While in and out of *Treasure Island*
The fair people of Dublin went
And the cold winter's day that it dryly was
Wore a shivering smile.

Since they had been at *Treasure Island*
I must have been in Dublin but I was not and nor were they –
At moments such as that
We are the treasure no island has the humour to conceal and
     make at home.
Otherwise in other days we would not be the outsiders to each
     other that we are.

# Note to a Team Manageress

Woman, you believe your husband is a poet
Yet you wonder what is the matter
When after an attempt to mountain-climb
He has no heart to natter.
You wonder also why the hell so
Why your husband is not first man in the band.
I say, how else can it be when his wife
Carpets the atmosphere with sinking sands
Instead of seawaters the mind's feet need?
Rake sleep for him to land in:
Then he may break the record for the high jump.

# In Memoriam Brendan Behan

This man though he had played the fool
Had been down at Song – at the edge of that bitter pool
Under a yew tree riven by a long sharp sun
He had stood and Death the Savage had stayed true to him.
The Savage Death changed back the man into a boy
And under a Holiday Saturday Summer sky
He lay on Dollymount Strand. Like a virgin girl
In his soft white massy flesh and his brown curls
But the proud nose bespoke the rock-stepping boy.
The crowds went about their play
As though he weren't there, giving him the freedom
Of their battered carnival mind. He was their son.
So it was until there chanced upon the *plage*
A small boy of forty years of age
In sailor gear from Beauchamp Place.
Among the people he looked not of their race
Yet he was not from outer space
But from the glossy forests of Rathgar.
He had tucked in his belt a pen-knife for
Tickling little old ladies on the 44.
This now he flourished and then scooped a hole
In the sleeping giant's side (the body's soul)
And in that hole he made a nest
In which he danced and danced for lust
(And money) and declared that he had found
The secret to the singer's life and round
And round London and Paris and New York
He flew, sucking on a spent cork.
Alas his fate was not what in Rathgar is done:
When the giant snored he disappeared as smartly as up a jumbo's
    arse.
And now Dublin may breathe freely for her son.

# To George Barker on His Sixtieth Birthday

In Spring my father goes to the wars
And in Summer he dies
But October brings him home.
It is only Winter that will not change
For we never can find the same gold twice.

# Combe Florey

*to Laura Waugh*

Wilderness that not always would deliver:
But to us come from the hot clink of London
It was Tel Aviv, the Hill of Spring and Garden of the Sea
To wake in the morning and to hear the stillness –
And that in spite or because of
The racket of birds – more than one
Woodpecker inhabited the oak outside my window
And at six each morning wound up their clocks in a loud
    manner
Not to speak of the woodpigeon, the cuckoo, the others
Whose names I do not know.
I said to the woman of the house in my own painful and boulder
    fashion:
It is a crying shame to be a creature of this earth
And not know the names of the birds in the trees
And yet I know the names of fifty motor cars.
She said: Lord, I do not think I know the name of even one of
    the little creatures.
And so saying, she gave tiny feet back to my boulder and pain.

V

# The Night They Murdered
# Boyle Somerville

As I was travelling one morning in an empty carriage
On a train passing south through the west
A small old woman with her husband who was smaller
Hobbled in, shut the door and sat down.
They told me they were going home to Skibbereen,
That they were old-age pensioners and proud of it
Enjoying free travel up and down the country.
They sat down opposite me and we conversed
When it suited us
Such was the ease with which we comported our silences.
Outside, the fields in their summer, lay on their sides in the sun,
Their season of flashing over.
Nor did we evade each other's eyes
Nor pronounce solutions to the awful war-in-progress
Except by a sign-language acknowledging
That here was the scar that lay *inside* the wound,
The self-betrayal beyond all chat.
And all this ease and all this sombre wisdom came
Not from me who am not by nature wise
But from the two old-age pensioners in their seventies.
He was a king-figure from out the islands of time,
A short round-shouldered man with a globe of a skull
Whose lips were the lips of an African chieftain
Having that expression from which there is no escape,
A gaze of the lips,
Interrupted only by the ritual blowing of an ancient pipe.
His wife – being a queen – told him to put away his pipe;
Did he not see the sticker on the windowpane?
It said NÁ CAITH TOBAC – but he did not hear her
No more than he heard the ticket inspector
Who having failed to draw attention to the warning notice
Withdrew apologetically, apologizing for the intrusion.

So, while the old man blew on his walnut plug
His wife gazed out the window and so did I.
When she spoke, she spoke of the old times and the *scoraíocht*
Back in Skibbereen and of the new times and the new words.
"Ah but," he interposed, glaring out into the blue-walled sky,
"I found out what was in it, and was not in it,
The night they murdered Boyle Somerville;
I knew then that it was only the sky had a roof."
Whereupon beads of sweat trembled on his upper lip
Between the black bristles of his pouring flesh.
Here was an old man, fit to humble death.

*1972*

# Ireland 1972

Next to the fresh grave of my beloved grandmother
The grave of my first love murdered by my brother.

# With Soldiers to Wait on Her While in Her Coffin Ride

Unarmed except for the
Fierce angry dandelions in their lapels
Two boys shot dead at point blank range
By troops.
In the dying summer sun
Britain Godiva rides through Derry streets
With soldiers to wait on her
While in her coffin ride

Penniless escape for a
Pale paper star pinned to a blue sky
A boy burnt to death
By a Big-Time Forty-Niner.
In the dying summer sun
America Godiva rides through Tipperary streets
With soldiers to wait on her
While in her coffin ride

*8 July 1971*

# Tribute to a Reporter in Belfast, 1974

Poets, is not this solitary man's own uniquely
Utilitarian technique of truth-telling,
This finely apparent effort of his
To split the atom of a noun and reach truth through language,
To chip-carve each word and report
As if language itself were the very conscience of reality –
A poetry more
Than poetry is.
Tonight once more he has done his work with words
And fish roots and echoes of all manner and kind
Did flower up out of an ocean-floor resonance
So rapidly but with such clarity
That you were made to look out of the eyes of another
Even as the other shot you dead in the back,
Out of the eyes of a Catholic republican
Whose grandparents were Quakers in Norwich,
But likewise out of the eyes
Of a seventeenth-century Norfolkman in Virginia
Sailing a copper knife through the soft pink air
Of an Indian's open mouth . . .

Gratias for the verbal honesty of Liam Hourican
In a country where words also have died an unnatural death
Or else have been used on all sides for unnatural ends
And by poets as much as by gunmen or churchmen.
Day and night his integrity of words has sustained us.

# Pulpit Bishop Sickness, AD 1973

He has carved out on his face an arch smirk,
An eternal catwhiskers of benign contempt
For rude humanity. Look how he swishes
Not his tail but his skirts
As from pulpit he condescendingly mews
That in the context of our civil strife
His denunciation of birth control should not be seen as political:
"Birth control is not in Ireland a political question."

Now as I watch this feline fabricator clutch claws
About the cerebral viscera of his sheep
I glance over at an aged companion
And see crucifixes of anguish crucify her face.
Through thick and thin – thin mostly –
She has stayed faithful to her church;
Yet daily the quick viciousness of prince cat
Cuts into her, makes of her daily life
A ritual in schizophrenia;
She has known nothing but dismay all her days
And now this last outrage – this sly wounding
Of all honour, truth, sense – fixes it
That she will go alone to her deathbed having known
Small love on this earth, not even from Christ's church.
Is not this *pangur dubh* – from whose dug-like eyes
Oozes vanity's green curdled vapour –
A knife in the face,
A knife in the ordinarily innocent face of life?

# The Limerickman that Went to the Bad

Well, fellas, as ye all know, I'm a Limerick stalwart
Who was chosen for the British Lions team for South Africa
And I went out there – but to play football not politics.
One night after a function in J–Burg
A Limerick exile came up to me and flung his maulers around
    me
And naturally I thought I was amongst one of our own.
But d'ye know what he said – looking funny-like out of his
    headlights –
He said: "I've just seen two young glorious African gentlemen
Playing handball in church."
And with that he deliberately poured his entire pint glass of lager
Over my head.
I was not surprised to find out later that he was a spoilt priest
And that no sooner had he landed in South Africa
Than he had started co-habiting with a coloured skivvy.
Like all Limerickmen that go to the bad he had a history.
But for sheer blasphemy, can you imagine anything more
    fucking blasphemous
Than two coloureds playing handball in church? Jasus.

# In Energy Alone Is Eternal Delight

Cardinals Cushing and Conway
Strolling in a stutter down the tarmac aisle
Of Galway Jail turned Cathedral;
The one enduring with antique dignity
The age-old cloud-grey hopelessness
Of the magnificently endless coming and
Going, day in, day out, of hangover;
The other solemn and cerebral
Putting out moral judgement on the old
Smiler from Boston, Mass.

# Dún Chaoin

*for Bob, Angela, and Rachel, in Nigeria*

I was standing at the counter
In a bar at the world's end.
The large weathered man behind it
Was more native to the place than the place itself.
His father's fathers . . .
A big blue man like that, I thought, could not be strange
With a stranger
So when he did not speak
An old fear whistled through me:
I am not welcome in this place.
I kept a grip on my pint glass
And my eyes to the left of me
Gripping the bay window and outside
The red sun at nightfall
In the same plane as the bar room
Descending the window pane.
Its going down took about as long
As it takes a boy or girl to climb down a tree.
Gone and not long after
I thought I could hear
A long-lost music long lost from the earth
And as I looked up from the counter, shaking my head,
The big man too was shaking his, birds and tears
Falling out of the rafters of his eyes. The both of us
Laughed and he turned up the volume
Of his openly concealed battered old wireless,
*Telefunken,*
And when we were going out he said: Good night
And may God bless you on the road.
I went out willing to sleep on mountainsides anywhere,
Fearing no man or beast, machine or mist.

# In Memorian Micky Duke

*for James Liddy*

Dusk plays cat chase cat
In and out the tall trees round his chalet
While, in the Far Away, the twin towers of Mullingar Cathedral
Play Constantinople in the snow light of twain.
Inside in the once teeming kitchen
Micky Duke sits down to breathe
And bear it and take off his shoes.
On the sea-blue dresser – still polished new –
A Woolworth's thimble sits right side up and shut
And yet –
Each silvery dint is as thronged and shining
As a window on the morning of the revolution.
He shall sleep in his wings with fire over mountains in his breast.

# Drug Swoops at Sligo Festival

It is under the moon late in the day on the shores of the huge
    Atlantic;
Two boys hotfoot from Dublin in trembling and joy in the cold
    backyard of a well-lit pub –
Cold but teeming with Peers and Contacts
And with the Plain People of Ireland.

The two boys wonder if they know a soul there who might lend
    them the price of a drink;
They are happy yet in their happiness is growing that terror born
    of the Holy Combination of Pennilessness, Love and
    Rebellion –
Mere youngsters, they have run away from home.

In silence staring at the sky pattern over Sligo Bay it is the same
    object that they see;
They cannot say what it is except that it has the exact same
    shape as has a wave of the sea
In a child's pencilled picture of a mythical ship – it has wings and
    is black.

The clearer it develops the more it flaps and flaps and tracks and
    zooms before them
Over all the inferno of the sky and devours them, leaving them
    standing there
Quite helpless and free . . .

Secretly they were glad to be in the garda barracks –
Soon they would be home – no abyss should last nor did they
    wish it to –
Yet such was the contempt with which their captors viewed
    them –
Bloody Women's Hair, Bloody Women's Blouses –

The two boys were filled with a new unease.
They were put, however, on the Dublin train in the
    morning . . .

Envoi, let us now fill the Powers for Law and Order
With a real unease; the two boys never for a moment guessed
That Sergeant Nixon had laid hands on them not for such sweet
    reason
As to mend the Flower of Generations but to find
What he was certain he would find but did not because they had
    not —
Ashes of hashish in a caftan's hem.

# Seer

I see now that we
Whom you call your mates
Are but so much stuff archly toyed with,
Cherished coldly,
You with your eyes on what people say about you
And with your ears on yourself in the mirror;
How, seer, you taste yourself
Like a fat sandwich between your tiny lips.

Here, seer, a saucer
For all your airs of creature
Love and eye's truth of laughter:
Pale night's near gone;
Sup up before it's green;
Or else by day be seen this once
For what you are:
Sleek meek spy cocked to pounce.

Should I or one of mine
Meet death this day
You would be here by midnight mewing out
Subtile sorrows, scraping round
Amongst the bottles,
Between slurped sups of speaking thieving
From truth-tellers their talk;
And your eventual spiel, seer, reek of the lair.

Behold you in your lair
After the event: a wat'ry sun
By Macgillycuddy Reeks
Spills, oozes, over you bent over
The screed of a stylish lie

Logically but through ordure conjured up;
As evil as a formula so this is.
No child of truth was ever preconceived.

You, seer, have deep need
To deliver offspring to their parents dead;
You are the midwife with the moustachioed smile;
The more helpless the victim the more sweet
Is death's taste to your ear;
You are the insider with a life outside
And an inside inside;
Your death wish to be drowned chewing out of your own paw.

# Petrie Petrie

The problem of being Colonel Petrie
In the slate house on Town Hall Hill
Bearing as he does the responsibility
Of being a fount of erudition –
Having to cultivate parson and curate,
Then annually to address the local Society
On the zoology of the Bible –
Is that not even the clippings, secretively inserted
At Genesis or the Psalms, of the nude
Stripper with her nipples like victims ringed
And her ponytail arrowed
And her lips daubed carmine with a felt pen
Can make Petrie Petrie:
Fetch me the tweezers Alice, I'd fain smile.

# The Day of the Starter

I have known Donal Dowd these forty years.
He may well be the biggest butcher in town
But I remember the day – and it breaks my heart
To contemplate it – when he was a messenger boy
Down in the abbatoir.
I may say, men, he is the same man
Today as he was forty years ago,
Except of course for the casa on the hill
His wife and six daughters.
Donal Dowd has given that woman everything – every
Conceivable gadget on this earth –
Walkie-talkie dish washer, clothes washer, carpet washer.
No, love is love: each
Morning as he starts the Rover 2000 with the automatic gears
He revs thrice for the wife.
She, beaming from the rear, shrieks after him into the exhaust:
"Oh, he's a perfect starter, he's my beau."

# The Girl with the Keys to Pearse's Cottage

*to John and Judith Meagher*

When I was sixteen I met a dark girl;
Her dark hair was darker because her smile was so bright;
She was the girl with the keys to Pearse's Cottage;
And her name was Cáit Killann.

The cottage was built into the side of a hill;
I recall two windows and cosmic peace
Of bare brown rooms and on whitewashed walls
Photographs of the passionate and pale Pearse.

I recall wet thatch and peeling jambs
And how all was best seen from below in the field;
I used sit in the rushes with ledger-book and pencil
Compiling poems of passion for Cáit Killann.

Often she used linger on the sill of a window;
Hands by her side and brown legs akimbo;
In sun-red skirt and moon-black blazer;
Looking toward our strange world wide-eyed.

Our world was strange because it had no future;
She was America-bound at summer's end.
She had no choice but to leave her home –
The girl with the keys to Pearse's Cottage.

O Cáit Killann, O Cáit Killann,
You have gone with your keys from your own native place.
Yet here in this dark – El Greco eyes blaze back
From your Connemara postman's daughter's proudly mortal face.

# Dr Plantagenet Higgins

His father was Higgins but Higgins is Higgins
So the boy had it changed to Plantagenet Higgins;
Now at Theatre Fitzwilliam quietly making a million
He performs as a peer of the psychiatric profession.

Meanwhile in the asylum there's a boy called Pat Browne
And slowly but surely they're putting him down;
He likes to make things, he's quiet, and he sings;
But – Pat Browne thinks he's Pat Browne – opines Plantagenet
    Higgins.

# Letter to Ben, 1972

*4 The Terrace, At The Ridge Of The Two Air-Demons, Co Leitrim*

It is half-past nine on a July night
The town's, and the emperor's, artillery are outside,
Are all perched up inside an ocean wave that's riding –
Along with the weed-adorned boards of sunlight, filthy jewels and
     millefiori refuse –
Sea breezes that themselves are riding into each other at right angles
Across this broken street we call *The Terrace*;
And there is grass growing in the sand and old Ben
Is stretched out happily in a sunny corner too – never again
Will he or I be a cause of fright to each other;
We're on the same side, just different sides of the ocean.

Come on up, Ben, take a seat in the gods,
The roof has at least three-quarters blown off,
Even the grey pools by the bridge cannot help
But be motherfathers to wildflowers
And all the wild animals too, including ourselves, the bear and the fox,
Whom tycoons thought to cage,
Have broke grave and cursed no one:
We know the mines will produce in their own time
Abundance:
Iron hills in the east
And gold in the northwest.

Oh such light from the east, Ben,
And it is only half-past nine on a summer's night.
Darkness has entered already the arena
Trampling the manure-larded sand and straw
With all her young splendour more bare and ebony than before;
Her ceremonial chains proclaiming no escape nor for the spectator.
So, in history, the ridge becomes deserted now and then:
Right now, just you and me, Ben, and the species.

# And that Being so

My soul is the High Meadow we played in,
My cousin and I, when we were young,
The High Meadow where we danced
Round a fairy ring.

My soul is the figure of my first love
Skipping quickly across the sands,
Her hair dyed yellow — was that wise? —
Round her laughing eyes.

But the High Meadow's been built upon
And that being so and my first love gone
My soul must step in the streets
Round the fire of song.

# Night of Nights

Veiled in movement like a stream, the dancer
of the dance of night, into the mind of Odin
like pools burnt out of rock she dances:
and she under sleep under bloodshot suns
in the house near a river of dark.

Dead, you tell her, dead, and the dead go
walking on, tall in their solitude:
O Odin, hear us: should no man die
from death, this night of nights.

# The X-Poet Sings to the Spirit of His Native Land

If time be really like the Dead Sea
(And no bird fly from coast to coast)
Then why not fill the Dead Sea in
With morality, cornflakes, decency.
Build an almighty culture stadium
For the clean-shaven and stenchless:
Fill the streets and hotels with models of purity
And put an end to evil and things like that:
Banish the sun from outer space
And arrange comprehensive night school for all:
Teach to gods below how to walk, how to talk,
How to accelerate drunkenly straight
On the crooked white line of Temperance,
How to make up, how to break love,
Tell on the truth and never say aye
To the worlds that stagger between me and you.
Roll out the red carpet, my dear,
I've come to bring progress to Hell.

# Lady and I

Day broke her water
For the race to run in pairs
Across the white-wine peaks
Of the cathedral hills:
Yet the pair of us stayed aground.

*We are afraid of heights,*
*Lady and I.*

Noon lay seaward
With a thousand flowers,
The sea riding free
In the comprehension of the sun:
Yet the pair of us stayed ashore.

*We are afraid of depths,*
*Lady and I.*

Night fall and what
Was I saying when I
Took up the bed and walked
Out of time
To eat with a snake in Tel Aviv?

*We are afraid of words,*
*Lady and I.*

# Animus Anima Amen

He went into a bar, feel deeply in love with a
strange girl, and said:

> Where did you come from?
> The moon.
> I bet *he* didn't like that.
> Who?
> Him.
> Who'se him?
> The man –
> In the bloody moon. Why didn't you say so?
> Katherine.
> Paul.

And he smiled. And she smiled. And they relaxed
in each other's arms for about a year or so. In the
end, she went back to the fellow in the bloody moon.

# The Unrequited

In the autumn evening light
She is combing back her hair.
In the autumn evening light
On a stool before the mirror
Making cold-as-ice streams
Of her yellow hair.
In the autumn evening light
She says: I do not love,
I do not love you, Paul.

In the noonday rain
Of winter, amongst working-men,
At the bar of a public house, I sit
Still as the stillness of the falling rain.
And I am pale and restless
And the working-men around me
Are pale and restless
As the stillness that is still
Like the stillness of the falling rain.

# To an Old Friend

You are a poet and a good man too
And would that more were of your kind
And took example from your rational pose
Down thirty years of song.

Strange, therefore, that you choose a public place
To make light of an unrequited heart
And, in the folly of your common sense, scoff
At the purple of a young man's pose.
I would not mock an old man making love
Nor scorn the affectation of the flower in bloom.

# The White Window

Of my love's body I think
That it is a white window.
Her clothes are curtains:
By day drawn over
To conceal the light;
By night drawn back
To reveal the dark.

# NOTES

20   *Taoiseach*: Irish prime minister.

42   *buachaillín*: Small boy.

59   *Boyle Somerville*: On 24 March 1936, at his home in Castle-townsend, Co Cork, Admiral Boyle Somerville was murdered by the IRA.

59   *NÁ CAITH TOBAC:* No Smoking.

60   *scoraíocht*: Visiting neighbours for festive gossip.

64   *pangur dubh*: Black cat.